X-Rated

SHOTS

More than 50 Shots We Dare
You to Say Out Loud

RUNNING PRESS
PHILADELPHIA • LONDON

A Running Press® Miniature Edition™
© 2004 by Topics Entertainment, Inc.
Shot glasses on cover © 2003 Kalan LP
All rights reserved under the Pan-American and
International Copyright Conventions
Printed in China

Library of Congress Control Number: 2003109768

ISBN 978-0-7624-1863-3

This book may be ordered by mail from the publisher.
Please include $1.00 for postage and handling.
But try your bookstore first!

Running Press Book Publishers
2300 Chestnut Street
Philadelphia, PA 19103-4371

Visit us on the web!
www.runningpress.com

Contents

It's All in the Name

Shots, shooters, slammers—
Whatever you call them, shots are
synonymous with uninhibited fun.
There's no sipping or savoring, no
sniffing or swirling, just toasting to
good times and good friends before
throwing 'em back. The very nature
of shots steps outside the bounds
of refined drinking, but there are
some concoctions that grab our
attention with more than their alcohol content. It's often a recipe's
naughty name that really gives a

shot its kick—and *these* are the shots we never forget, whether their titles make us gasp, giggle, or laugh out loud.

In these pages you'll find a sampling of the best X-rated shots around. So when at the bar ordering a round for you and your friends, or when at home showing off your own bartending skills, shake up your regular drinking repertoire with these scandalous drink sensations. Cheers!

The Basics

There aren't many rules when it comes to shots, but there are a few things you should note. The average shot is 1 to 2 ounces and should be drunk in one satisfying swallow. You can make shots individually or in volume, serving a group by simply maintaining the ratio of ingredients.

Certain shot recipes require more than just pouring the ingredients into the glass—for instance, you may need to **shake** or **layer**.

SHAKE: Pour the ingredients into a cocktail shaker filled with ice cubes, cover, and shake well to combine and chill the ingredients. Strain the mixture into the shot glass(es) and serve immediately. Don't shake recipes that call for one or more parts of soda—instead, mix these with a spoon to maintain the carbonation.

LAYER: A layering effect is possible due to the different densities of the ingredients. To layer, pour the heaviest ingredient into the shot glass(es) first, then add the lighter ones in the order given in the ingredients list. To ensure that the ingredients don't mix, after pouring in the first (heaviest) ingredient, add each additional ingredient by pouring it slowly over the back of a spoon.

Now on to the recipes!

RECIPES

69

1 part crème de banane
1 part anisette
1 part Irish cream

Layer in a shot glass.

ROUTE

69

©Kalan SG114 493593

Aggressive
Blow Job

1 part grain alcohol
3 parts cola

Mix with ice and strain
into a shot glass.

© 2003 Kalan LP www.kalanlp.com

Angel's Tit

1 part white crème de cacao
1 part heavy cream
Maraschino cherry

Layer the white crème de
cacao and heavy cream in a
shot glass. Chill for 30 minutes
before serving, and garnish
with a maraschino cherry.

A.S.S.

1 part Absolut® vodka
1 part mentholmint
   schnapps
1 part sambuca

Shake with ice and
strain into a shot glass.

Ball Hooter

1 part tequila
1 part peppermint schnapps
Beer, for serving

Shake the tequila and
schnapps with ice and strain
into a shot glass. Serve with a
short, cold glass of beer.

© 2003 Kalan LP www.kalanlp.com

Bikini Line

1 part vodka
1 part Tia Maria®
1 part raspberry liqueur

Shake with ice and strain
into a shot glass.

BLOW JOB

1 part Irish cream
1 part Kahlua®
Whipped cream

Mix the Irish cream and Kahlua
in a shot glass. Top with
whipped cream. Drink using
only your mouth—no hands!

© 2003 Kalan LP www.kalanlp.com

Body Shot

1 ounce vodka
1 sugar packet
1 lemon wedge

Recruit a member of the opposite sex
and lick his/her neck to moisten a small
area. Pour the contents of the sugar
packet onto the moistened area. Have
your partner hold the lemon wedge by
the rind (lemon flesh facing outward)
with his/her lips. In quick succession,
lick the sugar from your partner's neck,
shoot the vodka, and then suck the
lemon from his/her mouth.

BOOTY JUICE

1 part Midori®
1 part coconut rum
1 part spiced rum
Splash of 151-proof rum

Shake with ice and
strain into a shot glass.

CAUTION CAUTION CAUTION CAUTION

CAUTION: OBJECT IN PANTS IS LARGER THAN IT APPEARS

© Kalan SG247

CAUTION CAUTION CAUTION CAUTION

Brass Balls

1 part Grand Marnier®
1 part peach schnapps
1 part pineapple juice

Shake with ice and strain
into a shot glass.

Buttery Nipple

1 part butterscotch
    schnapps
1 part Irish cream

Shake with ice and
strain into a shot glass.

ALL GROWN UP AND STILL FASCINATED BY NIPPLES

620955 © Kalan SG220

CITRON MY FACE

2 parts Absolut Citron® vodka
1 part Grand Marnier®
1 part sour mix
Splash of lemon-lime soda

Shake with ice and strain into
a shot glass.

Cunnilingus

1 part Irish cream
1 part peach schnapps
2 parts pineapple juice
Whipped cream

Shake the Irish cream, peach
schnapps, and pineapple juice with
ice and strain into a shot glass. Top
with whipped cream.

© 2003 Concept & design from bCreative.com

Death by Sex

3 parts vodka
1 part Southern Comfort®
1 part amaretto
1 part sloe gin
1 part triple sec
2 parts peach schnapps
Splash of orange juice
Splash of cranberry juice cocktail

Shake with ice and strain
into shot glasses.*

*Because this recipe includes many ingredients,
it's easier to make in volume, about 6 shots.

Fiery Kiss

1 shot (1 to 2 ounces)
  cinnamon schnapps
1 to 2 drops clover honey

Mix the schnapps and honey
in a shot glass. Coat the rim
of the shot glass with honey,
if desired. Use more or less
honey to taste.

Flooze Booze

1 part Jägermeister®
1 part root beer schnapps

Shake with ice and
strain into a shot glass.

FReNCH KiSS

1 part Irish cream
1 part white crème de cacao
1 part amaretto

Layer in a shot glass.

FUZZY NIPPLE

1 part vodka
1 part peach schnapps
1 part orange juice
Splash of triple sec

Shake with ice and
strain into a shot glass.

Fuzzy Screw

2 parts vodka
1 part peach schnapps
1 part triple sec

Shake with ice and strain into
a shot glass.

GENERATION SEX

3 parts Pepsi® cola
1 part coconut rum

Mix with ice and strain
into a shot glass.

621060 © Kalan SG22

Golden Nipple

1 part Goldschläger®
1 part butterscotch schnapps
Irish cream, to fill

Shake the Goldschläger and
schnapps with ice and strain
into a shot glass. Add the Irish
cream (up to 1 part) to fill the
shot glass.

G-Spot

1 part Southern Comfort®
1 part raspberry liqueur
1 part orange juice

Shake with ice and strain
into a shot glass.

HEAVENLY BODY

1 part pear liqueur
1 part Frangelico®
1 part Irish cream

Layer in a shot glass.

There's too much **blood** in my alcohol system.

558817 © Kalan SG136A

© 2003 Kalan LP www.kalanlp.com

Hialeah Hooker

1 part strawberry liqueur
1 part cognac
1 part vodka
1 part rum

Shake with ice and strain
into a shot glass.

HONEY-DEW-ME

2 parts Bärenjäger®
1 part melon liqueur
4 parts orange juice

Shake with ice and
strain into a shot glass.

Illicit Affair

1 part Irish cream
1 part peppermint schnapps
Whipped cream

Layer the Irish cream and
schnapps in a shot glass, and top
with whipped cream.

Irish Kiss

1 part Irish cream
1 part peppermint
schnapps

Shake with ice and
strain into a shot glass.

©Kalan SG108 428292

I ALWAYS TAKE LIFE WITH A GRAIN OF SALT

A SLICE OF LIME AND A SHOT OF TEQUILA

597484 © Kalan SG151

Kick Me in the Jimmy

1 part Jägermeister®
1 part whiskey
1 part tequila
1 part cinnamon schnapps

Shake with ice and strain
into a shot glass.

The Lucky Stud

1 part Metaxa®
1 part Galliano®

Shake with ice and strain
into a shot glass.

I'm not as
think as you
drunk I am.

558809 © Kalan SG135A

© 2003 Kalan LP www.kalanlp.com

Mother Pucker

2 parts vodka
1 part Dekuyper Sour Apple
  Pucker Schnapps
Splash of club soda
Splash of lemon-lime soda

Shake with ice and strain
into a shot glass.

Naked Navel

**2 parts chilled vodka
1 part chilled peach schnapps**

Chill both bottles of liqueur
in the freezer. Pour the vodka
into a shot glass, then pour
in the schnapps. The schnapps
will form a ball in the bottom
of the glass.

NASTY BITCH

**3 parts chilled tequila
1 part chilled Cointreau®**

*Chill both bottles of
liqueur in the freezer.
Mix in a shot glass.*

Nutcracker

1 part Kahlua®
1 part Irish cream
1 part amaretto

Shake with ice and
strain into a shot glass.

ORGASM

1 part white crème de cacao
1 part amaretto
1 part triple sec
1 part vodka
2 parts light cream

Shake with ice and strain into
shot glasses.*

*Because this recipe includes many ingredients,
it's easier to make in volume, about 6 shots.

Pants on Fire

1 part banana liqueur
1 part grapefruit juice
1 part orange juice
1 part strawberry liqueur
1 part vodka
Splash of half-and-half

Shake with ice and strain into
shot glasses.*

*Because this recipe includes many ingredients,
it's easier to make in volume, about 6 shots.

Panty Raid

2 parts citrus vodka
1 part raspberry liqueur
Splash of lemon-lime soda
Splash of pineapple juice

Shake with ice and strain
into a shot glass.

ONE DRINK,
I FEEL GOOD.
TWO DRINKS,
I FEEL
EVERYONE.

Rat BasCard

626036 ©Kalan SG266
©2002, Concept & design from bCreative.com®

© 2003 Concept & design from bCreative.com

PIERCED
BUTTERY NIPPLE

1 part Irish cream
1 part butterscotch
   schnapps
1 part Jägermeister®

Layer in a shot glass.

The Pink Panty

1 part vodka
1 part cinnamon schnapps
Splash of cranberry juice cocktail

Shake the vodka and the cinnamon
schnapps with ice and strain into
a shot glass. Add a splash of
cranberry juice cocktail.

Purple Hooter

1 part raspberry liqueur
1 part lemon-lime soda
1 part vodka

Mix with ice and strain
into a shot glass.

Don't tease me if you can't please me!

625988 ©Kalan SG264

© 2003 Kalan LP www.kalanlp.com

Screamer

1 part gin
1 part rum
1 part tequila
1 part triple sec
1 part vodka

Shake with ice and strain
into shot glasses.*

*Because this recipe includes many ingredients,
it's easier to make in volume, about 6 shots.

SEX ON THE BEACH

1 part vodka
1 part peach schnapps
1 part cranberry juice cocktail
1 part grapefruit juice

Shake with ice and strain
into a shot glass.

Shake That Ass

1 part blue curaçao
1 part banana liqueur
1 part sour mix
1 part orange juice

Shake with ice and
strain into a shot glass.

S.H.I.T.

2 parts sambuca
2 parts Häagen-Dazs®
  Cream Liqueur
2 parts Irish Mist®
1 part tequila

Shake with ice and
strain into a shot glass.

SICILIAN KISS

1 part amaretto
1 part Southern Comfort®

Combine in a shot glass.

Silk Panties

1 part peach schnapps
3 parts vodka

Shake with ice and strain
into shot glass.

Sliper'N'Nipples

1 part Irish cream
1 part sambuca

Layer in a shot glass.

Slippery Nipples

**1 part Kahlua®
1 part Irish cream
1 part peppermint schnapps**

Shake with ice and strain
into a shot glass.

REMEMBER
MY NAME, YOU'LL
BE SCREAMING
IT LATER

© Kalan SG188

© 2003 Kalan LP www.kalanlp.com

SLUT JUICE

8 ounces vodka
3 ounces orange juice
1 tablespoon lemonade
   mix

Mix in a 12-ounce glass,
stirring well. Serve in 6
to 8 shot glasses.

Warm Blonde

1 part Southern Comfort®
1 part amaretto

Layer in a shot glass.

White Mess

1 part white rum
1 part crème de cassis
1 part root beer schnapps
1 part coconut rum
1 part heavy cream

Shake with ice and strain
into shot glasses.*

*Because this recipe includes many ingredients,
it's easier to make in volume, about 6 shots.

Women's Revenge

1 part crème de menthe
1 part Irish cream

Serve each ingredient in a separate
shot glass. Take a sip of the crème
de menthe. Without swallowing the
crème de menthe, take a sip of the
Irish cream. Gargle, and swallow.
Repeat to empty the shot glasses.

X

1 part amaretto
1 part strawberry
  schnapps
Splash of sour mix
Splash of cola

Shake with ice and
strain into a shot glass.

Index

Photography Credits:

Shot glasses courtesy of Kalan LP,
and photographed by Gilbert King.

Black Box/ Retrofile: pp. 60, 85, 93, 99, 111

Camerique/ Retrofile: p. 89

Corry/ Retrofile: p. 40

DeBrocke/ Retrofile: pp. 80, 103

Laenderpress/ Retrofile: p. 36

Photomedia/ Retrofile: pp. 55, 107

R. Block/ Retrofile: pp. 13, 32

Retrofile: pp. 20, 39, 43, 47, 49, 67, 71, 75, 90

This book has been bound using handcraft methods and Smyth-sewn to ensure durability.

The dust jacket and interior were designed by Alicia Freile.

The recipes were provided by Paul Knorr.

The text was edited by Katie Greczylo.

The text was set in Block, Bulldog, Brush Script, Egyptienne, and Garage Gothic.